Evelyn and Duck Duck
Go to the Zoo

For Evelyn
My inspiration and my Joy
With love

- Nana

To my dear Friend Jackie
whose written words made it a joy to
illustrate and bring to life

- Brenda

PS: Brenda says "look out for the snails?"

In a small town, on a winding road, in a cute house, lived a little girl called Evelyn. She lived there with her Mummy, Daddy and Prickles the hedgehog.

Evelyn was very happy in her house. It was full of love, laughter and joy and she could not think of anywhere else she would rather be. She had a beautiful room to sleep in with animals painted on the wall and lots of toys to play with. They were her friends.

There was little Ted, Gilbert the giraffe, big dog Woof, Flip flop bunny and rag doll Daisy. And then there was Duck Duck. Duck Duck was Evelyn's best friend. She loved him sooo much.

One day, Evelyn was reading a story to her friends when Mummy and Daddy came to join her.
"Come on Evelyn" they said, "let's go to the Zoo".

"Yippee" said Evelyn as she scooped up Duck Duck "you must come too. We're going to the Zoo".

At the Zoo Evelyn and Duck Duck saw lots of wild animals. First, they saw a Lion. The Lion had a loud **ROOAAR** when he said hello.

Evelyn held onto Duck Duck very tightly.
"That Lion is too noisy" she said.
Duck Duck gave her a wink and a smile
and Evelyn was not worried any more.

Behind the big iron railings Evelyn and Duck Duck saw a huge Elephant with giant feet. The Elephant was stomp, stomp, stomping around the pond and the ground shook.

Evelyn had to give Duck Duck a big squeeze. "Be careful", she said to Duck Duck. "I don't want you to get crushed".
Duck Duck gave her a wink and a smile and Evelyn was not worried any more.

Around the corner and up the hill were the cheeky monkeys, chattering, swinging and playing and having so much fun. Evelyn laughed and laughed at the Monkeys' happy games.

She picked up Duck Duck and swung his arms like the Monkeys in the trees. Duck Duck and Evelyn were having so much fun.

"I think the Penguins need feeding." said Mummy.
"How exciting" said Evelyn, "shall we go see, Duck
Duck, shall we go?"

What a noise! The penguins were all lined up, honking and flapping, jumping and splashing and trying to get the next fish. Evelyn clapped and clapped and clapped. "Look Duck Duck, they are soo hungry". Duck Duck agreed, was that his tummy rumbling too?

After the fun and games Evelyn was hungry too. The Café smelled good. Fresh bread, pasta, crisp apples and scrummy muffins. Evelyn gave Duck Duck a big hug "don't worry" she said, "we won't forget your worms".

Far too soon it was time to go home. Tucked up in her car seat Evelyn gave Duck Duck a big hug and with a warm smile and a twinkle in her eye she whispered, "I did like seeing all the animals in the zoo, but I am so happy you live with me...". With that, Evelyn and Duck Duck were fast asleep dreaming of new adventures and promising to be best friends forever.

**Goodbye
until next time**

Printed in Great Britain
by Amazon